fast fun & easy

FABRIC BAGS

10 Projects to Suit Your Style

C&T PUBLISHING

Text © 2005 Pam Archer
Artwork © 2005 C&T Publishing, Inc.
Publisher: Amy Marson
Editorial Director: Gailen Runge
Acquisitions Editor: Jan Grigsby
Editor: Cyndy Lyle Rymer
Technical Editor: Sara Kate MacFarland
Copyeditor/Proofreader: Wordfirm
Cover and Book Designer: Kristy K. Zacharias
Page Layout Artist: Kirstie L. McCormick
Composition Services: Happenstance Type-O-Rama
Illustrator: Kirstie L. McCormick
Production Assistant: Matthew Allen
Photography: Diane Pedersen and Luke Mulks, unless otherwise noted
Published by C&T Publishing, Inc., P.O. Box 1456, Lafayette, CA 94549

Front cover: crown jewels (page 41), easy evening elegance times two (page 29), knitting and crafts/market bag (page 53), to-go gift bag (page 36), toting possibilities (page 45) all by Pam Archer

Back cover: a day around town (page 49), to-go bag (page 37), your calls are covered (page 25), needle case (page 55), and toting possibilities (page 59) all by Pam Archer

Library of Congress Cataloging-in-Publication Data

Archer, Pam Kincaid.
 Fast, fun & easy fabric bags : 10 projects to suit your style / Pam Archer.
  p. cm.
 ISBN 1-57120-302-8 (paper trade)
 1. Handbags. 2. Tote bags. 3. Sewing. 4. Fancy work. I. Title: Fast, fun, and easy bags. II. Title.
TT667.A73 2005
 646.4'8—dc22
         2004017493

Printed in China

10 9 8 7 6 5 4 3 2 1

Dedication

This book is dedicated to my wonderful family: my husband, Mike, and my sons, Scott and Brent. Without your love, support, and encouragement, this book would have been an insurmountable task.

To my parents, for their leadership by example: Dad, for his perseverance and pursuit of excellence; Mom, for being a wonderful role model and my best friend. You both *always* encouraged me to pursue my love of color, texture, and fabric.

Acknowledgments

To the C&T family: Cyndy Lyle Rymer, Sara Kate MacFarland, Diane Pedersen, Jan Grigsby, and Amy Marson—thank you all for your words of wisdom and support during this creative endeavor.

Jean Chandler, for your unconditional friendship, candor, "therapeutic" walks, and awesome desserts.

Karen Dye, for being so supportive and for helping me stay connected with the real world while I was in "book mode."

Sarah H. Lajoie, for your friendship, love of all things creative, wonderful sense of humor, and beading expertise.

Marsha McClintock, for your friendship, humor, and generous creative support. You have a magical touch in connecting people with the right environment.

The Portland "Dream Team," a fabulous group of well-known fabric artists that I am honored to be a part of. Gratitude abounds for your shared insights, expertise, and support.

And a special thank you to Linda Griepentrog—without your instrumental direction and mentoring, this book would only be a dream.

Contents

Introduction

My journey with bags actually began with a wrong fabric purchase. A co-worker asked me to pick up some fabric for her home office. After I described it to her, I closed with a funny remark, "Don't worry, if you don't like it, I can always use it for a handbag." The remark itself is not unusual; what was unusual was that after 35-plus years of sewing, I had only made a couple of handbags.

I gave in to that small internal voice and very soon, I was in the "bag" business, creating specialty bags for crafts and marketing, bags for gift giving, and handbags for day or night. Before long, the bags were selected for juried art shows, which opened a door to a whole new, wonderful way of sharing my experience and love of bags—through writing.

Making bags is fun and a fabulous way to express yourself. *Fast, fun & easy fabric bags* is just the book you need to make your own one-of-a-kind bag. This book is a guide to understanding what makes a quality bag. It also provides information about selecting fabric, interfacing, and "findings" (page 10) that will make your bag great. In addition, you'll discover three different ways to construct a bag, directions for making your own handles, and information about closures. A materials list for each project includes ideas for easy embellishment techniques for added touches. From there, simply select one of the ten available projects, and get ready to sew. You'll quickly learn that fast, fun, and easy bags are just as practical as they are appealing.

So, go "shop" your stash or the store, then have some fun and make a bag!

getting started

A handbag or tote bag serves many purposes, but a bag's most important qualities are function and style. It's key to understand what makes a quality bag.

Handbag Anatomy 101

Knowing the functions of parts of a bag provides a solid framework for making a bag that will wear well. A bag's exterior fabric distinguishes its appearance. Often, a bag needs a certain amount of ease, provided by gussets. The lining offers durability and a finished appearance, while the unseen interfacing gives the bag its stability. Interior or exterior pockets provide convenience and organization. The handles make for easy "tote-ability." A closure for security often adds to the bag's look.

Fabric Choices

With all the wonderful fabrics available today, the fabric selection process might seem a bit overwhelming. However, once you apply the following three steps, you will discover that it's easier than you thought.

1. **Consider the function of the bag.** Ask yourself *how* the bag will be used. Is it intended for daytime business use or special occasions? Is it an all-around bag you'll use every day? The bag's purpose provides clues for the type of bag to make and for the best choice of fabric. For example, an evening bag of silk dupioni would be a great choice; canvas, however, would be out of place in the evening. Likewise, using silk for an everyday tote would not be a good choice.

2. **Select a look you like.** As important as knowing the bag's purpose is being aware of what styles you like. Go through magazines and catalogs, and clip pictures of bag styles you like. After a while, you will notice a pattern emerging. Sometimes, that pattern is a certain shape, size, or color. Look for the similarities in your clippings to lead you to the right fabric and style combination.

3. One of the most fun steps is actually shopping for your fabric. As you review the fabric options and their qualities, keep in mind the bag's purpose and your preferred style.

☐ Functional fabrics take everyday wear and tear in stride.

Canvas: the queen of functionality

Cotton: offered in a kaleidoscope of patterns and colors, quilted or not; heavier-weight home dec fabrics work well

Denim: hard-wearing twill weave available in assorted weights and colors

Light upholstery: durable and available in a variety of colors, patterns, and textures

Nylon: known for its vast assortment of colors and durability

☐ Fashion fabrics offer an additional element of texture. They may require special handling, but it's worth it! Try sueded rayon.

☐ Pile fabrics have wonderful texture and a definite one-way or directional feel (nap). If you use pile fabrics, be sure to cut all pieces in the same nap direction, unless you vary it for a special effect.

Chenille: offered in a great selection of patterns and colors with a tactile dimension

Corduroy: rich piles with ridges cut into the fabric

Faux fur: fabulous fakes in every pattern nature has to offer

Suede cloth: knit or woven, both with a wonderful sense of texture

Ultrasuede: the best version of real suede

Velvet and velveteen: luxurious texture and color play

☐ Specialty fabrics are a bit more challenging to work with but are worth the extra time for a dressier look.

Metallics: a fabulous shine and dimension (Use a metallic needle, and change it often. Stitch carefully—needle holes are usually permanent.)

Pleather: sews like a dense knit (As with metallics, needle holes are permanent.)

Silk dupioni: High luster, great texture, but frays easily (Add an extra ¼˝ to your seam allowance.)

Satin: high luster and a bit slippery (Keep lots of pins handy.)

Ultraleather: like the real thing, but much lighter (Needle holes are permanent.)

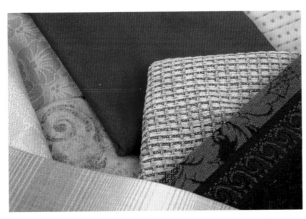

Sampling of the wonderful fabric choices available

One of the benefits of making a bag is the ability to incorporate your preferences for fabrics and personal requirements for a usable bag.

Before You Cut

When you purchase fabric, check the end of the bolt, and note the care recommendations. Prepare your fabric in the same manner that you will care for it once it's made into a bag. Run washable fabrics through a full wash-and-dry cycle, using normal detergent. Take dry-clean-only fabrics to a professional cleaner before constructing your bag. Prewashing helps get rid of any excess dye and eliminates subsequent shrinkage with later care.

Support System

Interfacing adds support to the bag's body, preserving its shape and helping it withstand wear. The bag's style and fabric selection determine its support requirements. Let's take a look at some of the bag stabilizers available.

sew-in interfacing

Interfacings that are sewn into the bag provide hidden stability, because they aren't visible from the bag's exterior. Napped fabrics, for example, require a sew-in interfacing to provide the required strength. Sew-in interfacings are either woven or nonwoven.

☐ Nonwovens—such as felt, Pellon, and stiff interfacing—range from soft to ultra-firm.

Softer bags that require less structure, but need added strength do best with a lightweight interfacing. A more structured bag made with upholstery fabric needs the firmness and support of stiffer interfacing.

☐ Woven—options span from buckram to canvas—give your bag a tailored, sculptured look.

fusible interfacings

Fusible interfacings adhere to the fabric because one or both sides, as with fast2fuse (see Resources, page 64), has been coated with a layer of adhesive that is activated by the heat from an iron.

Fusible interfacings, which add substance to bags that require more body than what is provided by sew-in interfacing, come in a range of weights, from sheer to very dense. A heavier interfacing adds more thickness to a lightweight fabric; adding a heavier interfacing to a heavyweight fabric makes it hard to sew.

testing

Where and when to interface? The most important rule is *always test first!*

Watch for two things: Does the interfacing show through to the right side of the bag? Is the interfacing firm enough? A fusible interfacing may seem like the best choice until you try it on a silk and discover a residue on the right side of your fabric. A lightweight nonwoven may seem like a good stabilizer for a chenille bag until you discover the bag won't stay upright because of its weight.

Coordinate the interfacing color with the bag color as closely as possible. Nothing is more disheartening than interfacing that shows through or that has changed the color of your fabric.

Apply the interfacing to the *entire* bag body, facings, and the fabric handles (if you are making them). The best time to apply the interfacing is immediately after cutting out your bag. This step immediately prepares your bag for construction and provides a convenient place to adjust your interfacing. If your bag is still wobbly, add a second layer. If your bag is too stiff, you can opt for a lighter-weight stabilizer.

It is said that form follows function, and so it goes for bags. From soft and pliable to rough and rugged, today's bags can be made in every size and shape imaginable. Make sure you have tested and applied the right stabilizer to help your bag retain its shape and durability.

To Line or Not to Line?

The answer is simple: Line your bag. Lining your bag adds a finished appearance. The lining should complement the bag's body in weight and durability.

Because the lining is both durable and smooth, it takes the stress of all that is carried in the bag and makes sure nothing gets caught on the inside.

fun!

Linings offer a secure, out-of-the-way place to add a pocket or two. When selecting a lining, choose wisely and test it. Like interfacings, a bag's lining needs to be compatible with the rest of the bag.

easy!

A structured bag needs a heavier lining; use a lighter lining for a lighter bag.

Self-fabric makes a wonderful lining. Making a bag out of denim and lining it with the same denim makes a very consistent and sturdy look. If a self-fabric gives the bag more body than you like, try using a sturdy cotton in a contrast color for some added personality.

Linings add personality to a bag.

tips for choosing a lining fabric

☐ Look closely at the yarns that make up your bag's fashion fabric to see what colors have gone into it. Use those colors as a springboard for selecting a coordinating lining.

☐ Use a color wheel or the 3-in-1 Color Tool (see Resources on page 64) for ideas on how to put together successful color combinations.

☐ Leftover scraps or an abandoned project can make a most wonderful lining. Avoid dark-colored linings. Lighter colors make it easier for you to find your purse's contents. A black leather wallet shows up readily against a red lining but not so readily against a black lining.

A lining adds the strength and durability the bag requires and provides the finishing creative touches that make it unique.

Facings

Not all bags require a facing, but more structured bags benefit from the addition of a facing along the upper edge. Applying a lightweight interfacing to the wrong side of the facing adds stabilization at a key stress point (the bag's opening), lends needed reinforcement, and gives your bag a more professional look.

Pick a Pocket

Ever met a pocket you didn't like? They are a welcome addition to any well-made bag.

Which pocket style is best? The answer depends on your bag style, fabric selection, and personal preference.

☐ A *zippered pocket* on the outside or inside of the bag offers added security. If you don't need or want the security of a zippered pocket, consider a basic open pocket style, such as a flat or pouch pocket.

☐ A *flat pocket* can be made simply by folding under a ½″ hem on a fabric rectangle, then stitching it to your lining, leaving an opening at the top or side. Flat pockets can be self-lined or interfaced for added strength and finish.

☐ A *pouch pocket* is very similar to the flat pocket but offers a bit more security. This pocket has additional width at its top edge, with elastic added to provide some security once an item is placed inside.

So whether zippered, flat, or pouch, lined or unlined, pockets provide an important function in a well-made bag. Just pick a pocket and sew! (See page 18 for more information.)

Findings

Findings from A to Z

Findings refers to all those additional bag parts, from appliqués to zippers. Here's a short list of bag findings and their applications.

☐ Appliqués and beads offer decorative embellishment.

☐ Buttons and buckles can be both decorative and functional.

☐ Chains, cords, and handles attach to the bag's side or top to offer a convenient carrying option.

☐ Eyelets and grommets not only add interesting texture but are also functional for lacings and drawstrings.

☐ Magnetic snaps create a secure closing.

☐ Purse feet protect the base from wear and tear.

☐ Purse frames give a clutch bag a solid framework for closing.

☐ Rhinestones and trims add decorative touches.

☐ Rings connect handles to the bag.

☐ Zippers provide secure pocket and bag closures.

Remember that fabric selection and tote style help determine which findings to use.

Get a Grip

The right handle prolongs the life of your bag. Clutches often have no handles, so some have an optional chain that can fit inside the bag. Choose short handles for hand carrying; medium handles for slipping over the arm; and long handles for carrying over the shoulder.

ready-made handles

Handle options

In today's handbag market, there is a plethora of handles to choose from. Check out your fabric store or online for readily available handles in all sorts of materials, including wood, plastic, acrylic, bamboo, rattan, beaded, or metal. The handle's size determines where it is placed on the bag. Handles made from chains, cording, leather strips, beaded necklaces, and old belts offer a bit more flexibility for their placement. For unique handles, scout out garage and tag sales and thrift stores—you can even raid old handbags for their parts.

custom handles

So, how do you handle the handle? That's part of the fun. Purchased handles dictate their placement, because the size is predetermined. Handles that you make offer more flexibility for positioning. Both custom and ready-made handles can attach to the top or side of the bag to support and balance the weight. Select a handle that will enhance the look of the bag, give it balance, and enable it to handle the weight of the contents.

Custom-made handles, which can be flat or corded, offer the most versatility in length and size. A flat handle is fabric that is turned, reinforced with interfacing, and then highlighted with edgestitching. A corded handle is made by sewing fabric around a piece of cotton cording. It often has a light interfacing applied to help it turn to the right side. (See page 16 for instructions.)

Finding Closure

Bag closures fall into two categories: sewn or applied. Sewn-in closures include snaps, zippers, rings, drawstring cords, buckles, self-fabric loop and buttons, and hook-and-loop tape/fasteners. Sewn-in closures offer an easy, effective way to make sure your bag is secure.

Applied closures, such as grommets, eyelets, snap fasteners, and magnetic closures, usually require a small tool for easier application. When adding applied closures, follow the old adage of "measure twice, cut once." Remember, once you have made a hole, the location is set—or you have to do some creative embellishing to change it.

Care for Your Bag

To extend the life of your bag and the enjoyment you get from it, follow these simple tips.

When your bag gets dirty, clean it. That goes for the inside, too. Sometimes a little spot cleaning will carry you a long way. If you prewashed your fabric before making your bag, then you know it's safe to launder.

easy!

Coffee or tea stains on your bag? Try a little dishwasher detergent. It works on your food stains in the dishwasher, right?

Basic rubbing alcohol works well to remove ink and grease spots. Just make sure you test it in an inconspicuous spot first!

Repair snags and trim loose fibers; your bag will look all the better for it.

When the bag is not in use, stuff it with tissue or plastic bags to help retain its shape.

Speaking of stuffing, if you put more items in your bag than you have space for, then it's time to make a bigger bag. Filling your bag beyond its capacity will weaken seams, distort its shape, and shorten its life span.

Today, bags are available in a range of styles and colors. By applying the basic information from this chapter, you'll be able to create a bag that suits your purposes with the look, color, fabric, and findings that are perfect for your style. Your well-put-together bag will be durable, look professionally finished, and have just the right handles. Isn't that what a good quality bag is all about? Let's get started.

fast
fundamentals

Making a great bag is easier than it looks! There are several basic techniques to guide you through creating your own fast, fun & easy fabric bags. Once you've mastered these techniques, you'll be able to mix and match the bag's bottom style with handle styles and fabric options.

From the Bottom Up

After applying the interfacing to all the bag pieces and trimming the excess, you begin the bag's construction from the bottom up. Three different bag bottom techniques are available.

bottomless bottom

This technique is the easiest. There are two methods for making this bag style. The first consists of taking a long piece of fabric and folding it in half. The sides are then sewn together to form a folded, one-piece bag. The second is the box bottom. The beauty of the bottomless bag is that it can be closed by either rolling or folding it and then securing it with a tie, snap, or hook-and-loop fastener.

How-To's

folded, one-piece bag

1. Cut the bag and lining rectangles. Fold the bag in half with right sides together, matching the upper edges.

2. Pin the side seams together. Stitch, then press the seams open. Clip the corners, and trim the seam allowances to ¼″. Turn the bag right side out.

3. Press the upper-edge seam allowances under to the wrong side ½″, and fuse in place.

4. Repeat Steps 1–3 to make a lining.

5. With right sides of the lining together, slip the lining into the bag, aligning the side seams. Pin and edgestitch the upper edges together.

fast!

In a hurry? Fuse the upper edges together.

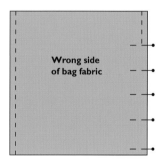

Pin and stitch sides.

Edgestitch around top of bag.

box bottom

This is one of the simplest ways to give a bag depth. Sew together a front and a back bag piece, with diagonal stitching across the bottom/side seam corners to create a boxlike bottom.

1. With right sides together, pin the bag front to the bag back at the lower edge. Stitch the seam, and press it open.

2. With right sides together, pin and stitch the front piece to the back piece along the side seams. Press the seams open, but do not turn the bag right side out.

3. Match the side seam to the bottom seam at each corner of the bag to form a point. Make sure the seams are aligned exactly. Pin securely to avoid shifting.

4. Stitch ¾″ from the point across the corner.

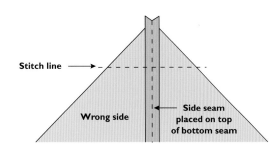

Point for box bottom

easy!

The further the seam is from the point at the corner, the wider the bag bottom becomes. Want a bag with less depth? Take a smaller seam across the point.

5. Trim the corner seam allowances to ¼″.

bottom wrap

This bag's construction includes three pieces—a separate bottom piece attaches to the long lower edge of a front and a back piece. The front and back pieces then wrap to the shorter side of the bottom, where they are all stitched together; hence the name.

1. Center the lower edge of the bag front along the long edge of the bottom piece, with right sides together. Pin in place and stitch, stopping ½″ from each end of the bottom edge. Clip to the last stitches on the bag's body *at both sides*. Press the seams open. Repeat for the other side.

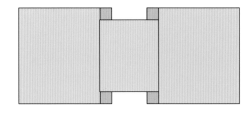

Lower edges stitched

2. With right sides together, pin the bag front and back side seams together. Stitch and press the seams open.

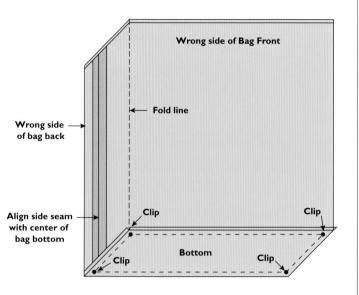

Wrap sides

3. Center the side seam along the short end of the bag bottom. Pin in place. Stitch across the short end.

4. Clip the corners, and trim the seam allowance to ¼″. Turn the bag right side out.

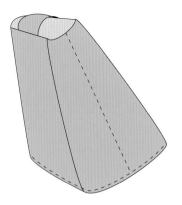

Bag turned right side out

Handle With Care

A good handbag shines when it has a well-done handle. The quality of the handle's application can quickly distinguish it as either well-made or home-made. So, although the bag's body is important, the handle is equally so. The handle is part fashion statement, part function, and part comfort.

You can find purchased handles in the notions department of your favorite fabric store, but don't forget to check tag sales, resale shops, and online resources, too. Before you begin your hunt, know the style you plan for your bag, how you intend to use your bag, and the bag's dimensions.

Ready-made handles come in a variety of colors, styles, and materials, ranging from bamboo to wooden, from beaded chains to leather straps. All ready-made handles come in *specific* sizes. Do your homework, so when it comes time to apply the handles, they'll be a perfect fit.

Bottom Technique	Handles	Closure	Fabric Options
Bottomless bottom	Chain	Hook-and-loop	Denim
	Corded	Magnetic snap	Silk
Bottom wrap	Wood	Ties	Home dec
	Beaded	Flap	Sueded rayon
Box bottom	Flat	Zipper	Pleather

Sewn handles offer more flexibility in terms of size, length, and placement. An added plus to making a corded or flat handle is that it can be made from the same fabric as your bag, or a coordinate if you prefer.

corded handles

Corded handles, made with fabric and cotton piping, are a good choice for any bag that you will carry by *hand*. Piping comes in a wide range of diameters and is usually found in the home decorator department. These handles are most commonly applied in a seamline, usually at the bag's upper edge.

1. Determine the desired length of your finished handle, plus seam allowances. *Double* this length to determine the amount of cotton piping you will need for each handle. Cut the doubled length in *half* if you're making 2 handles.

2. Cut bias fabric strips to cover the handles, using this formula: Cut strips the length of the handle(s), and the width should be 4 times the piping's *circumference* (distance around). Make sure the bias strip easily covers the piping and includes a ½″ seam allowance.

easy!

When using piping ½″ or larger, add extra seam allowance for easy sewing.

fast!

To help handles turn easily and to prevent unraveling, fuse a lightweight interfacing to the wrong side of the bias fabric strip.

3. Beginning in the center of the piping length, wrap the bias strip aound the cord, placing the right side of the fabric against the cord. Pin and baste across the short end at the midpoint. Pin along the remainder of the strip.

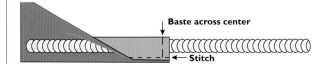

Corded handle started

4. Using a zipper foot, stitch down the entire length of the bias strip, taking care *not* to catch the piping in the stitches and using a ½″ seam allowance.

easy!

If you need a stiffer handle or if your stitches aren't close enough to the cord, leave a wider seam allowance to provide built-in filler.

5. Trim the seam allowance to ¼″.

6. Begin to turn the handle by sliding it over the other half of the piping cord length.

7. With the handle right side out, undo the basting stitches at one end. Retract the cord ½″ and trim. Repeat for the other handle cord. Baste across the finished handle ends.

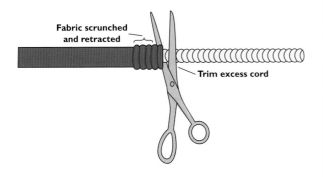

Retract fabric and trim cord from each end.

fast!

When you need handles in a hurry, substitute colored cording from the home decorator department in place of sewn handles. Just be sure to prevent unraveling by keeping the ends taped until they are securely sewn in place.

flat handles

Flat handles can be made in a variety of widths, fabric choices, and lengths. These handles work best for shoulder straps and are usually placed at either end of the bag. Flat handles offer several placement options. For example, use them with D-rings or with buttons.

1. Cut bias fabric strips in the handle length desired, plus seam allowances for each end, and double the desired width, plus 1″ for seams.

2. Fuse lightweight interfacing to the wrong side of the handle strip.

3. With right sides facing, fold the bias strip in half lengthwise. Pin and stitch using a ½″ seam.

4. Press the seam open. Trim the seam allowance to ¼″.

5. Turn the handle right side out, forming a long tube. Center the seam to the back of the handle. Press in place. Repeat for the remaining handle.

6. Cut a handle length of waistband interfacing, such as heavyweight Pellon or stiff interfacing. Trim ⅛″ from a long edge.

easy!

For added comfort, cut a piece of lightweight, nonwoven interfacing 3 times the width of the handle by its length. Wrap the handle insert (interfacing/Pellon) in the strip like a burrito. Baste through all layers in the middle, then insert the interfacing in the handle's opening.

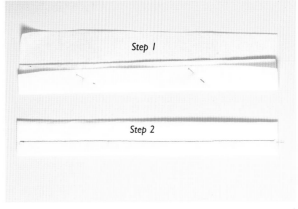

Burrito handle

7. Feed the handle stabilizer through the handle tube. Trim ½″ length from each short end.

8. Edgestitch the handle length, and baste across the short ends.

Edgestitch handle.

easy!

If your sewing machine isn't up to sewing through multiple layers of thick fabric, stitch a buttonhole at the end of the handle where the stabilizer has been removed. Make the buttonhole, tuck under the raw handle ends, and fuse the ends in place. Sew a button on your bag to attach the handle.

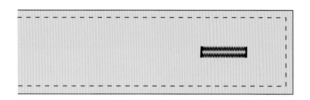

Buttonhole at end of handle

Pretty, Perfect Pockets

patch as patch can

No matter what the size or shape, patch pockets fly together with the greatest of ease. Just remember, the fold becomes the top edge of the pocket.

1. With rights sides together, fold the pocket in half, matching the raw edges. Pin around all 3 sides, leaving a 2˝ opening for turning.

easy!

If you're making a larger pocket, leave a bigger opening; a smaller pocket requires a smaller opening.

2. Using a ½˝ seam allowance, stitch the pocket edges. Trim the seam allowance, and clip the corners.

3. Turn the pocket right side out. Press. Tuck the remaining raw edge inside the pocket opening, closing it when the pocket is attached to the bag.

4. Edgestitch the pocket to the interior or exterior of the bag.

Pocket edgestitched in place

zippedy doo dah!

A zippered pocket offers a hidden, more secure pocket. It's easy to place a zippered pocket in the seam, either between the facing and the lining or between the bag and the lining.

To apply a zippered pocket in the seamline:

1. Cut the pocket the length of the zipper tape, and double the desired finished depth.

2. Align the pocket raw edge with the edge of the zipper tape. Stitch together. Repeat for the other side.

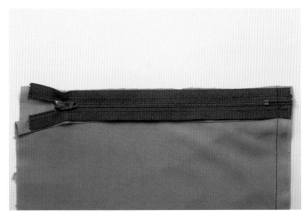

Align zipper to raw edge placement.

3. Center the zipper along one side of the bag facing. Place the pins in the facing to mark the start and stop of the zipper.

4. Staystitch the facing, using a ½˝ seam allowance between the pins at the lower edge. Clip the facing at the pins. Press under the seam allowance between the pins.

5. Position a long edge of the zipper adjacent to the folded edge of the facing. Pin in place.

6. Using a zipper foot, stitch the edge in place, leaving the zipper teeth exposed.

Zipper placement to folded facing

7. Repeat Steps 3–6 for the upper edge of the lining. Make sure the lining side seams match the bag seams.

8. Match the lining and facing clips. Pin. Baste in place.

9. With right sides together, pin the lining to the facing. Topstitch around the entire opening, starting and stopping at the clips.

10. Stitch the pocket side seams together from the clips, ending at the pocket fold and keeping the lining and facing free.

fast!

Instead of a zipper closing, use hook-and-loop tape as an alternate closure. Either a length of the tape or several hook-and-loop dots will keep the pocket contents in place. Applying a bead of fabric glue to the wrong side of the hook-and-loop tape, in addition to the stitching, will keep the tape secured.

Applying for Closure

Keeping the contents of your bag safe and secure is important. Bags can be readily secured by adding a tie, a snap (sewn or magnetic), a flap, hook-and-loop tape, a button and loop, or a zipper. The trick is to plan ahead for the type of closure you want. Closures such as magnetic snaps, zippers, flaps, ties, or even simple loops are inserted during construction, before a bag gets its facings or linings. Grommets, sew-on snaps, and hook-and-loop tape can be added when the bag is done. Knowing your closure of choice can make its application a snap!

easy!

5 tips for successful closures

1. Before inserting a magnetic closure, apply a piece of firm interfacing ½˝ larger than the snap at the spot where you will apply it. Some magnetic snaps are very strong, and without additional support, they will distort the bag's shape. Apply a magnetic snap before applying the facing, and center it along the upper edge of the bag for a polished closing. If the snap is applied to the bag facing, the extra bulk can make attaching the facing a bit tricky. Start pinning the facing from the center where the snap is, out to the sides, adjusting it to fit at the side seams.

2. Add a simple flap to the top of your bag. Cut out 2 of the desired shapes, interface, sew, and turn. Then insert the flap in the upper bag seam or topstitch it to the bag back. Fold the flap to the bag front, securing with a magnetic snap, sew-on snap, or hook-and-loop tape.

3. Ties and loops are the easiest closures to make. See page 16 for cording instructions. Make 1 loop for a loop-and-button closure, or make 2 ties with or without the cording. Insert the tie in the center of the bag's upper edge before adding the facing.

4. A double row of stitching where flaps, loops, or ties are applied provides additional stability and reinforcement.

5. Apply a small circle of lightweight interfacing to the wrong side of a button, toggle, or sew-on snap location to provide support to the fabric.

Today, bags are available in a wide range of styles and colors. By using the information in this chapter, mixing the different ways to build a bag, and choosing different handle options and closure styles in a variety of fabrications, you'll have a never-ending assortment of bags to sew. It's like a handbag smorgasbord!

bottle dressing

Special events call for celebrating! Why not "dress" the bottle accordingly? Within half an hour, your bottle can go from everyday to *extraordinary*.

COMPLETED WINE BAG: 6¼″ x 13½″

What You'll Need

- ☐ ½ yard organza, Fabric 1
- ☐ Optional: ½ yard organdy for contrast lining, Fabric 2
- ☐ 1 yard 1½″-wide wired ribbon
- ☐ 3″ beaded tassel
- ☐ Seam sealant
- ☐ Tracing paper
- ☐ Ruler
- ☐ Optional: 20″ bead wire, 26 or 28 gauge

How-To's

cutting

1. To create the pattern, draw a rectangle 15½″ × 6¾″ on tracing paper. On a long edge, place a mark at 10″. Use a small plate to create a curved edge that starts at the mark and ends at the 15½″ point on the opposite side; or, use the pattern on page 24.

Note: The 10″ edge is placed on the fold for cutting.

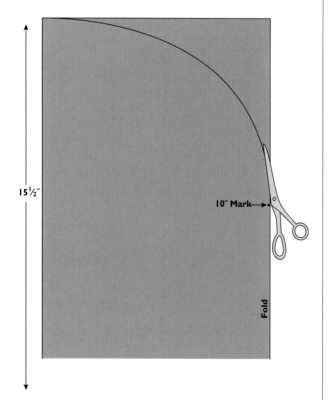

Create a curved edge.

2. Cut out 2 bag pieces: 1 from Fabric 1 (bag, piece A) and 1 from Fabric 2 (lining, piece B).

If you are not using a contrasting fabric, cut 2 pieces from Fabric 1 and mark them A and B.

easy!

To make a larger bag, measure the bottle at its widest point and add ¾″ for ease, plus the seam allowance. To accommodate a deeper bottle, sew a deeper seam at the corners of the box bottom.

sewing

Note: All seam allowances are ½″, unless otherwise stated.

1. Fold piece A with right sides together. Pin the long back seam. Stitch. Repeat for piece B. Press the seams open. Trim the seam allowance to ¼″.

2. Slip piece B into bag A with right sides together. Align the curved edges and the front. Pin the lining to the bag.

3. Stitch using a ¼″ seam allowance. Press the seams open. Trim the seam allowance to ⅛″. Clip the curves.

4. At the front corners, apply a drop of seam sealant. Let dry. Clip diagonally into the corners. Turn the bag right side out, and press the curved seam flat.

5. Turn the bag lining side out. Treating all layers as one, make a box bottom (see page 14).

6. Turn the bag right side out. Slip the bottle into the bag.

7. Slip the beaded tassel onto the ribbon half way. Position the ribbon at the neck of the bottle, aligning the beaded tassel with the curved opening in the bag front. Tie the ribbon into a bow.

easy!

Add some whimsy and texture by gluing a fun trim around the curved top of the bag.

fun!

Add strength and shaping capabilities to the bag's top seam by starting with a lightweight beading wire: With the bag wrong side out, lay the wire on the upper edge seam allowance. Starting at the front, use a 2.0-wide zigzag stitch to sew the wire in place over the seam allowance, stopping at the other side. To keep the wire ends from poking through the fabric, curl the ends around a straight pin and trim off the excess.

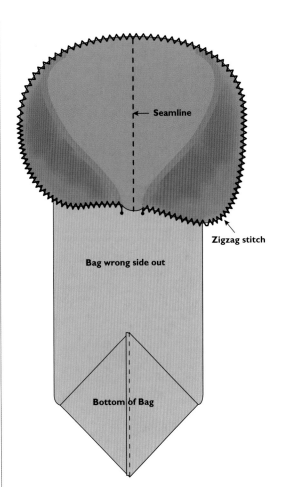

Wire up some fun.

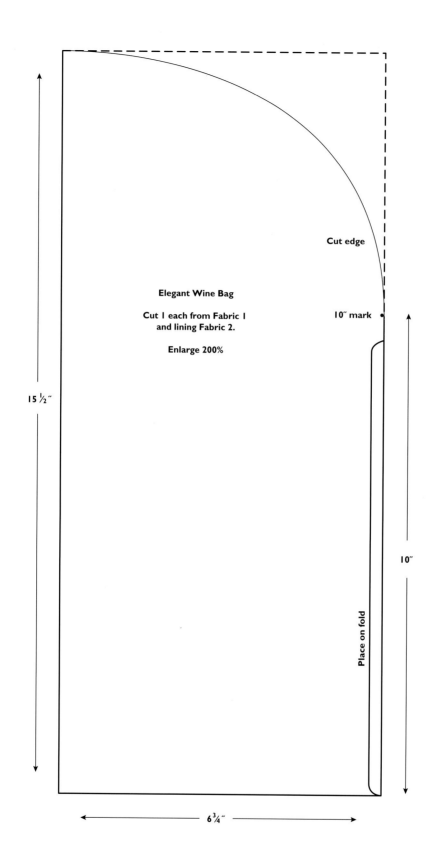

Elegant Wine Bag

**Cut 1 each from Fabric 1
and lining Fabric 2.**

Enlarge 200%

Cut edge

10″ mark

15 ½″

10″

Place on fold

6 ¾″

your calls
are covered

Keep your cell phone padded and well-contained with this easy one-hour project. Never miss a call again with this convenient loop slipped on a bag handle or belt.

FINISHED SIZE: 3½″ x 4¾″

What You'll Need

- ⅓ yard Fabric 1 for cover's exterior and flap's interior
- ⅓ yard Fabric 2 for cover's interior and flap's exterior
- ⅓ yard fusible knit interfacing
- Hook-and-loop fastener
- Matching thread
- Tracing paper
- Ruler

How-To's

cutting

1. To create the pattern, draw a rectangle 5½″ × 10½″ on the tracing paper. Fold the pattern in half lengthwise, creating a fold line in the center, 5¼″ from each end. At one short end, measure in ½″ from each side. Draw a straight line down each side to the fold line. Draw a line from the fold to the lower corners, creating a diagonal line. Cut your pattern along the lines you've drawn.

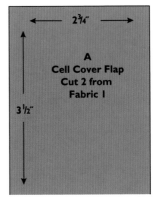

Cell cover flap A

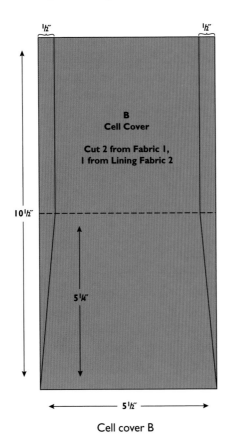

Cell cover B

2. Cut 2 cell cover B's: 1 from Fabric 1 and 1 from Fabric 2.

3. Create the flap pattern by drawing a rectangle 2¾″ × 3½″ on the tracing paper.

4. Cut 2 flap A's: 1 from Fabric 1 and 1 from Fabric 2.

5. Cut interfacing: 1 for cover B and 1 for flap A.

6. Cut 1 bias strip 1¾″ × 4″ from Fabric 1 for loop.

fusing

Fuse the interfacing to the wrong side of bag B, Fabric 2, and then to the wrong side of flap A, Fabric 1.

sewing

Note: All seams are ½″, unless otherwise stated.

1. With right sides together, pin the A flaps together. Stitch around 2 long edges and 1 short edge. Trim the seam allowance to ¼″. Clip the corners.

2. Turn the flap right side out, and press. Topstitch around the 3 sewn edges.

3. With right sides together, pin together the long edges of the loop. Stitch using a ¼″ seam allowance. Turn the tube right side out, and press the seam to the center back side. Edgestitch the sides.

← Edge stitch

Turn the tube right side out and edgestitch.

4. Fold the loop in half with the seamed sides facing. Baste the short ends together.

5. Center the loop, with raw edges matching, to the right side of the upper edge of Fabric 1. Baste in place.

easy!

To locate the center quickly, bring the side edges together and finger-press to form a crease. Repeat for the other piece. Line up the creases, and pin in place.

6. Center the flap over the loop with right sides together, sandwiching the loop. Baste in place.

Center the flap at the upper edge.

7. Pin the cell cover B pieces at the lower edge with right sides together. Stitch. Press the seam open.

8. With right sides facing, pin the long edges of Fabric 1 to the long edges of Fabric 2. Stitch. Trim the seam allowance to ¼″.

Stitch around 3 sides.

9. Pin the upper edges together. Stitch across the upper edge, 1″ from each corner.

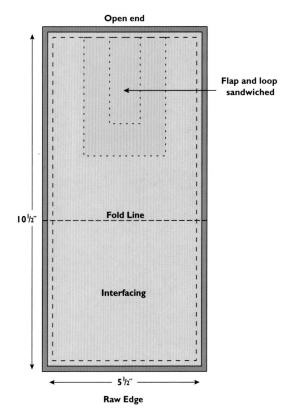

Stitch 1″ from each end at bag top.

10. Trim the seam allowance to ¼″. Clip the corners. Turn the cover right side out, and press.

easy!

Fuse a small piece of fusible web to match up the corners and edges. This keeps all the pieces in the right place for fast stitching.

11. Tuck the open seam allowance inside. Pin and topstitch along the upper edge.

12. Bring up the bottom edge, folding the cover in half to enclose Fabric 2. Match to the upper edges, and pin the side seams. Using a ¼″ seam allowance, stitch the sides closed.

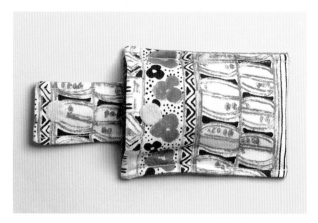

Bring bottom to meet top edge.

13. Apply hook-and-loop fastener to the wrong side of the flap and the right side of the cell cover.

easy!

For additional support, add a quick round of hand stitches to the hook-and-loop fastener.

Variation

Change the dimensions of the pattern to make a stylish case for your personal data assistant. Use fast2fuse to fuse the 2 layers together, and just satin stitch the edges. Easy!

3¼ x 3¾ finished

easy evening elegance
times two

Here's an easy, elegant, reversible bag to make in just a couple hours. The best part is that as you're making the bag, the "lining" becomes a second bag. Here's your chance to add a wild second fabric for the lining. Twice the bag for the time and effort of one!

FINISHED SIZE: 9″ x 5½″

What You'll Need

- ☐ ⅜ yard Fabric 1
- ☐ ⅜ yard Fabric 2
- ☐ ¼ yard fusible fleece

Note: Use fusible fleece with adhesive on only one side.

- ☐ 16˝ beaded handle
- ☐ Seed beads (for a 4˝ string)
- ☐ Beading needle
- ☐ Beading thread
- ☐ Two ⅝˝ buttons to cover

For maximum coordination, try to find a handle that has both fabric colors in it.

How-To's

cutting

Cut 2 bag pieces each from Fabric 1 and Fabric 2 using the pattern on page 31. Cut 4 bag pieces from the fusible fleece.

Cut a 1⅞˝-diameter circle for each covered button.

fusing

1. Trim ½˝ from the edges of the fusible fleece.

2. Fuse the fleece to the wrong sides of the 4 bag parts.

sewing

Note: All seam allowances are ½˝, unless otherwise stated.

1. Make 2 box bottom bags (see page 14), leaving a 4˝ opening in the lower-edge seam of bag B, Fabric 1, for turning.

2. With right sides together, slip bag A, Fabric 1, into bag B, Fabric 2. Stitch the upper edges of the 2 bags.

3. Trim the seam allowance to ¼˝. Turn the bag right side out through the opening, and press.

4. Topstitch the bag's upper edge.

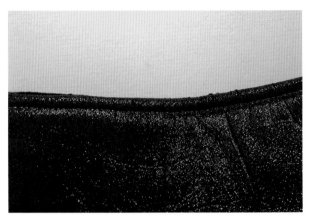

Bag stitched together at top seam

5. Slipstitch the opening in bag B, Fabric 2 to close it.

Instead of sewing the opening closed, use narrow fusible web to close it.

6. Hand stitch the beaded handle to the bag at the upper edge side seams.

7. Make the covered buttons, following the manufacturer's instructions, and stitch them back-to-back at a center upper edge of the bag, 1″ in from the edge.

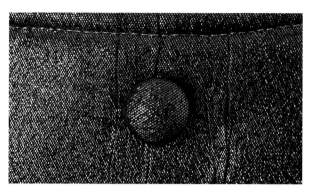

Position button 1″ from edge.

8. To form the loop closure, thread the needle with a double strand of beading thread. Beginning at the middle of the side opposite the buttons, string 4″ of seed beads. Anchor the beads in the bag's upper edge, next to the starting point, to form a loop. Knot the thread to secure.

easy!

For added strength, run the threaded needle back through the bead strand a few times before knotting.

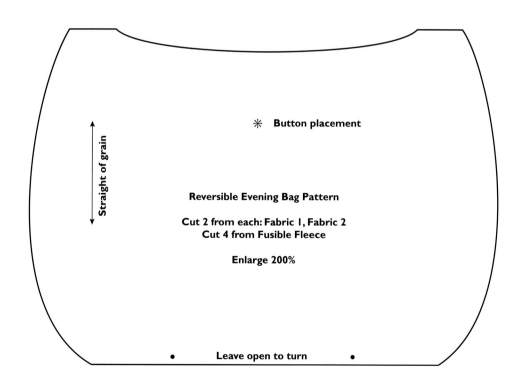

Straight of grain

✳ **Button placement**

Reversible Evening Bag Pattern

Cut 2 from each: Fabric 1, Fabric 2
Cut 4 from Fusible Fleece

Enlarge 200%

• **Leave open to turn** •

purse-onal pod

Eliminate bag clutter with this handy personal pod. Large enough to house your credit card, lipstick, a few dollars, and change—even your keys can find refuge in here. This bag can slip into the pocket of your favorite bag, and can be sewn in half an hour with the greatest of ease.

FINISHED SIZE: 7½″ x 4″

What You'll Need

- ☐ At least 12″ x 11″ scrap for Fabric 1
- ☐ At least 12″ x 11″ scrap for Fabric 2
- ☐ At least 12″ x 11″ fusible fleece

Note: Use fusible fleece with adhesive on one side only.

- ☐ At least 12″ x 11″ paper-backed fusible web
- ☐ Matching thread
- ☐ 4″ length of hook-and-loop tape
- ☐ Tracing paper

How-To's

cutting

To create the pattern, draw a rectangle 10″ x 9″ on tracing paper. Follow the diagram to add additional lines and measurements. Trim the corners, as shown, slightly rounding the points at the top and bottom to create a soft curve rather than a point; or, enlarge the pattern on the next page by 400%.

Use the pattern to cut 1 pod each from Fabric 1, Fabric 2, the fusible fleece, and the fusible web.

Cut the hook-and-loop tape in half, lengthwise.

fusing

1. Trim ½″ from the edges of the fusible fleece.

2. Fuse fleece to the wrong side of Fabric 1.

3. Fuse adhesive web to the wrong side of Fabric 2. Let cool and remove the paper backing. Fuse Fabric 2 to the fleece side of Fabric 1, forming a single fabric "sandwich."

sewing

Note: Use a ½″ seam allowance, unless otherwise stated.

1. Finish all the edges with a narrow zigzag stitch or by serging.

2. Center and stitch the hook side of the hook-and-loop tape on a long edge of Fabric 1. Center and stitch the loop side of the hook-and-loop tape on the opposite side.

fast!

3. Fold right sides together along the fold line. Use a ⅝″ seam allowance to stitch 1″ from each end. Note that the stitching meets the inside ends of the hook-and-loop tape. Press the seam open.

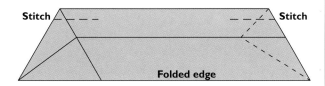

Stitch 1″ in from each end.

4. With the short ends right sides together, bring the center of the rounded point to meet the center seam. Pin in place.

Short ends meet to form a curved triangle shape.

5. Stitch the seams. Clip the corners, and finger-press the seams open.

6. Turn the pod right side out. Press.

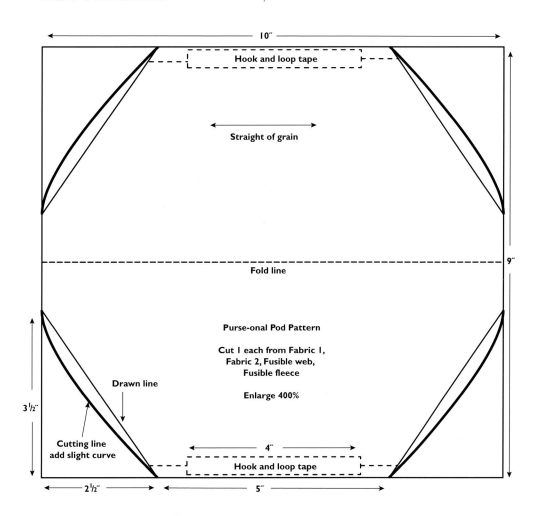

to-go bags

This is the quintessential bag for people on the go. Its chameleon-like qualities are perfect for any occasion. Need a stylish lunch bag? Sure, no problem! How about a quick handbag with Asian-inspired flair? Easy! A special gift bag? You've got it! Whatever you need, this bag can quickly be made in a couple hours.

FINISHED SIZE: 6″ x 9½″

What You'll Need

- ⅜ yard fabric, Fabric 1
- ⅜ yard lining, Fabric 2
- ⅜ yard insulation, Fabric 3 (for lunch bag only)
- ⅜ yard fusible interfacing (not needed for to-go gift bag)
- Thread to match
- Tracing paper
- ⅝″-round hook-and-loop dot

How-To's

cutting

1. To create a bag pattern, draw a square 11″ × 11″ on tracing paper. At one end, measure in ½″ from each side; mark. Draw a line from the mark to the opposite corner to create a diagonal line.

2. Use the pattern page 30 for the to-go lunch bag to cut 2 each of the following: main, Fabric 1; lining, Fabric 2; insulation, Fabric 3; and interfacing. Cut 1 5″ × 7″ bottom rectangle from each fabric (1–3) and interfacing.

3. To create a bag flap pattern, draw a rectangle 5″ × 6¾″ on tracing paper. Draw a horizontal line at 5″ from the lower edge. At a short end, measure in 2″ from each side; mark. Draw a line from the marks to the horizontal line to create a diagonal line; or, enlarge the pattern on page 40 by 200%.

4. For the to-go lunch bag flap, cut 2 from Fabric 1 and 1 from the interfacing.

fusing

Fuse interfacing to the wrong side of the bag's front, back, and flap pieces.

sewing the to-go lunch bag

Note: Use a ½″ seam allowance unless otherwise stated.

1. Create a bottom wrap (page 14) with Fabrics 1, 2, and 3.

2. Trim all seam allowances of the insulation to ¼″.

3. With right sides together, align the flap edges. Pin in place. Stitch around the sides, leaving the top edge open.

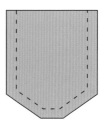

Stitch around the flap.

4. Turn the flap right side out, and press flat.

5. With right sides together and raw edges matching, center the flap to the upper edge of the bag back. Pin in place, and baste.

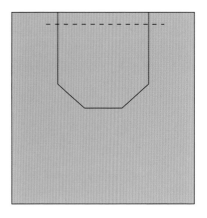

Center flap on back of bag.

6. Slip the insulation into the bag with the wrong sides facing.

Insert insulation into bag.

7. Follow the previous steps to prepare the lining, except leave a 4″ opening in one long bottom seam on one side.

8. Slip the bag (right side out) into the lining (wrong side out), matching side seams and raw edges. Pin in place.

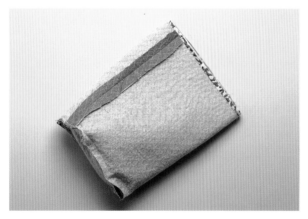

Slip bag into lining.

9. Stitch around the entire upper edge. Trim the seam allowance to ¼″.

easy!

If the insulation is thick, sew the lining together with a ⅝″ seam allowance.

10. Gently pull the bag through the opening in the lining. Edgestitch the lining opening closed.

11. Tuck the lining inside the bag, matching up seamlines. Pin in place. Hand tack the bag's lining to the bag's body at the bottom corners.

12. Press the upper edge of the bag, and topstitch ¼″ from the edge.

13. Position the hook-and-loop fastener carefully, placing the hook on the flap's underside and the loop on the right side of the bag where the flap rests. Hand stitch in place.

14. Press the bag and go.

fast!

For a bag that will have limited use, simply apply fabric glue to secure the hook-and-loop fastener.

variations

These examples can be made using the same technique as the lunch bag.

to-go Asian bag

1. Make the to-go bag following Steps 1–5 for the lunch bag, using the same fabric for self-lining. Trim the flap ¼″ on each side. Disregard the references to the insulation (Step 6).

2. Attach a frog closure and a beaded handle..

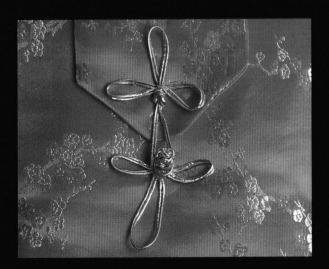

Add a simple strand of beads strung on wire to turn this to-go bag into a handbag!

to-go gift bag

1. Cut multiple layers of organza. (For a stiffer bag add more layers.) Cut 1 layer of netting. Layer the fabric, sandwiching the netting between the organza. Baste all layers together.

2. Apply decorative stitches and a variety of yarns. Machine embroider gift bag before assembling.

3. Make a to-go bag following Steps 1–5 for the lunch bag.

To stabilize the layers of fabric and for an unexpected touch, add a layer of decorative stitching and yarns to the right side of the bag's front, back, and top flap pieces.

4. Finish the bag by folding over the upper edge. Topstitch it in place. Use a small snap for the closure.

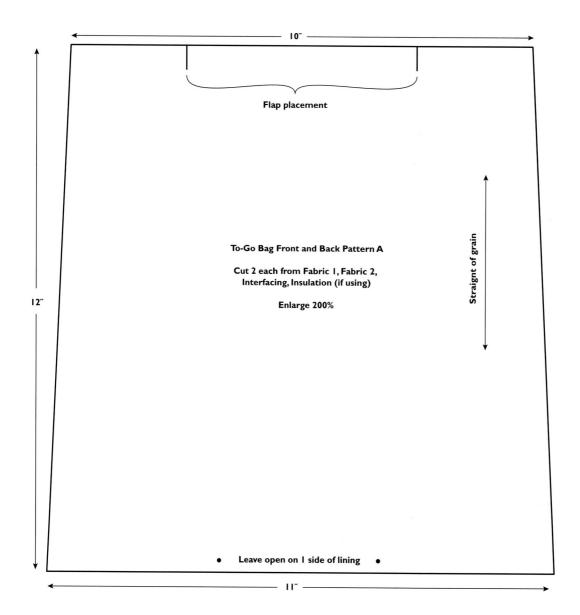

10″

Flap placement

12″

To-Go Bag Front and Back Pattern A

Cut 2 each from Fabric 1, Fabric 2,
Interfacing, Insulation (if using)

Enlarge 200%

Straignt of grain

● Leave open on 1 side of lining ●

11″

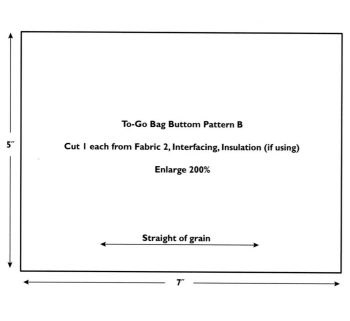

To-Go Bag Buttom Pattern B

Cut 1 each from Fabric 2, Interfacing, Insulation (if using)

Enlarge 200%

5″

Straight of grain

7″

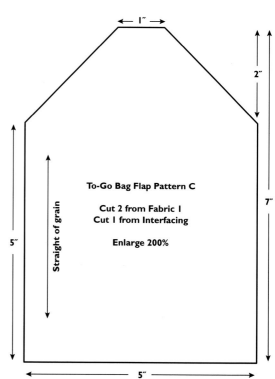

1″

2″

7″

To-Go Bag Flap Pattern C

Cut 2 from Fabric 1
Cut 1 from Interfacing

Enlarge 200%

5″

Straight of grain

5″

the crown jewels

Your jewelry will feel right at home in this convenient carrying bag. Complete with a ring roll, clear pockets for easy viewing, a polishing cloth for gentle care, and a zippered pocket, your valuables will be secure and will travel in style. All you need is about two hours to complete the bag.

FINISHED SIZES: Unfolded—10″ x 11½″, Folded—10″ x 3¾″

What You'll Need

- ½ yard Fabric 1
- ½ yard fusible interfacing, Fabric 2
- ⅓ yard polishing cloth, velveteen, ultrasuede, or chamois, Fabric 3
- 5″ × 11″ strip clear vinyl, Fabric 4
- 1 yard gold flat ribbon
- Seam sealant
- Fabric glue
- Fusible web
- 12″ length of ½″-diameter cotton piping
- 1″ hook-and-loop tape
- 9″ zipper

How To's

cutting

Cut a rectangle 11″ × 17″ from Fabric 1 and from Fabric 2.

Cut a rectangle 11″ × 9″ from Fabric 3.

Cut 2 rectangles 11″ × 2½″ from Fabric 4.

Cut 1 piece of gold ribbon 10″ and 1 piece 25″.

construction

Note: All seams are ½″, unless otherwise stated.

1. Fuse interfacing Fabric 2 to the wrong side of Fabric 1.

2. Press ½″ under to the wrong side at the lower edge of Fabric 1 and Fabric 3.

3. Fold the 25″ length of ribbon in half. Place the fold in the center of the upper edge of Fabric 1, matching the fold to the raw edge. Baste in place.

easy!

To prevent unraveling, add a dot of seam sealant to the ends of the ribbon trim.

4. Place Fabric 3 right side up, and position the Fabric 4 piece 1½″ below the upper edge. Use a paper clip at the sides to hold it in place and baste. Edgestitch across the lower edge of Fabric 4.

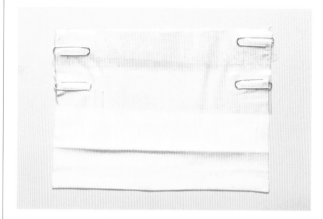

Vinyl pocket compartments

5. Stitch 2 vertical lines in the Fabric 4 strip 3¾″ from each long side to form compartments.

Detail of vinyl pockets

fun!

6. Place the top edge of the Fabric 4 strip even with the top edge of Fabric 3, overlapping Fabric 4 by ½″ to create a flap. Baste the top edges in place.

7. With right sides facing, pin Fabric 3 to Fabric 1, matching upper edges and side seams. Stitch 8½″ across the top and down each side. Trim the seam allowance to ¼″ and clip the corners.

easy!

8. Turn the bag right side out. Press the bag with care.

9. Turn bag inside out. With right sides together, bring the lower folded and pressed bag edge to meet the folded edge of Fabric 3. Pin the sides together. Stitch. Trim the seam allowance to ¼″, and clip the corners.

Bag wrong side out, prepared for zipper

10. Turn the bag right side out. Slip the zipper right side up into the opening between Fabric 3 and Fabric 1. Center the zipper on the folded edge of Fabric 3.

easy!

11. Leaving the zipper teeth exposed, pin the zipper in place.

Slip zipper in place.

12. Cut a length of fusible web, trimming the width to match the zipper tape. Leave the zipper teeth exposed, and sandwich the web between the folded-under edge and the zipper tape. Pin in place. Press to fuse.

13. Tuck the remaining zipper tape edge under the second folded edge of the bag, covering the zipper teeth. Repeat the fusing process for this side.

fun!

14. To make a ring roll, use the covered cording technique (page 16). Use a 12″ length of piping and a 4½″ × 9″ bias fabric strip.

15. Trim ½″ from each end of the piping. Tuck the raw edges on both ends inside the roll, and fuse it closed with a small piece of fusible web.

16. Cut a 1″ hook-and-loop tape in half. Position the hook tape at the end of the ring roll. Apply a dab of glue to each hook-and-loop tape piece. On the right side of Fabric 3, position the hook-and-loop tape 1¼″ from each edge and 2″ from the zipper.

variation

For a more casual look, make the crown jewels case using quilted cotton, batiks, or home dec fabrics.

toting
possibilities

This perfect shoulder bag begs for a trip to the farmer's market, a weekend get-away, or a workout at the gym. This bag features a zippered inner pocket for keeping valuables safe and separate from the rest of your must-have items. Make it and take it in a day.

FINISHED SIZE: 14″ (at base) x 23″ (at top of bag) x 12¾″

What You'll Need

- □ 1½ yards fashion Fabric 1 for bag exterior (1 yard if using 54″-wide fabric)
- □ ⅙ yard contrasting Fabric 2 for bag bottom
- □ 1¼ yards lining, Fabric 3
- □ 1½ yards fusible fleece

Note: Use fusible fleece with adhesive on one side only.

- □ 1 yard lightweight nonwoven interfacing
- □ 9″ × 13″ canvas
- □ 1 yard stiff interfacing
- □ 9″ zipper
- □ Matching thread
- □ Fabric glue

How-To's

cutting

Pattern A: Cut 2 each from Fabric 1, Fabric 3, and interfacing, using a crosswise grain layout.

Pattern B: Cut 1 each from Fabric 2, fusible fleece, and Fabric 3.

Pattern C: On fold, cut 1 from lining Fabric 3.

Cut 2 pieces 3⅛″ × 25″ of lightweight interfacing for the tote's upper edge (facing).

Cut 2 bias strips 3¾″ × 32″ each of Fabric 1 and fusible interfacing for handles.

Cut 2 pieces 1⅛″ × 32″ stiff interfacing for handle inserts.

Cut 2 pieces 4½″ × 13″ canvas for bag bottom.

Cut 1 piece 4½″ × 13″ stiff interfacing for bag bottom.

easy!

If you cut the fabric on the bias, as suggested for this tote, add an additional layer of interfacing on top of the fusible fleece to provide extra stabilization.

fusing

1. Trim ½″ from the side seams and bottom edges of the fusible fleece. Starting at the fold line on tote A, fuse the fusible fleece to the wrong side of the 2 tote pieces.

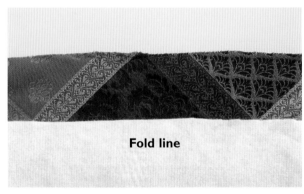

Fold line

Fusible fleece on fold line

2. Apply lightweight interfacing to the tote's facing.

3. Trim ½″ from the edges of the fusible fleece tote pattern B. Apply the fusible fleece to the wrong side of the tote's contrast bottom piece B. Fuse the interfacing to the wrong side of bag bottom B.

4. Fuse the interfacing to the wrong side of the bag's handles.

sewing

1. Construct a bottom wrap (page 14).

2. Make flat handles (page 17).

3. Matching raw edges, place one end of the handle right side down on the facing's right side, 5¾″ from the side seam. Pin the handle securely in place.

4. Stitch each handle to the facing on top of the edgestitching lines, stopping at the tote's fold line.

Handle stitched to facing

5. Prepare the lining following the same steps as for the tote's body, leaving a 6″ opening in the bottom seam, as indicated on pattern A.

6. Add a zippered pocket C between the handles (see page 19).

Zippered pocket pinned to folded edge

7. With the tote turned wrong side out, slip the lining with the right side out into the tote. Right sides will be facing each other. Match the side seams, the zipper opening, and the raw edges. Pin the lining to the tote facing.

8. Stitch around the entire facing. When you approach the zipper, change to a zipper foot so you can stitch closer to the zipper.

9. Reach through the hole in the bottom of the lining and pull the tote through to the right side.

10. Tuck the lining into the tote, ensuring a good fit.

11. With the precut canvas and stiff interfacing, make a "canvas sandwich" by placing the interfacing between the 2 layers of canvas. Machine baste all 3 layers together.

12. Apply a healthy layer of fabric glue at the tote's bottom. Insert the canvas through the hole in the lining. Let it dry completely before moving on to step 13.

13. Machine stitch the hole in the lining closed. Hand tack the lining to the tote at the bottom corners.

14. Press the tote, and topstitch 1½″ from the tote's upper edge.

See page 59 for a colorful variation of this bag.

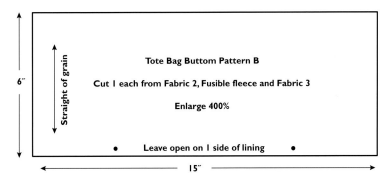

6″

Straight of grain

Tote Bag Buttom Pattern B

Cut 1 each from Fabric 2, Fusible fleece and Fabric 3

Enlarge 400%

Leave open on 1 side of lining

15″

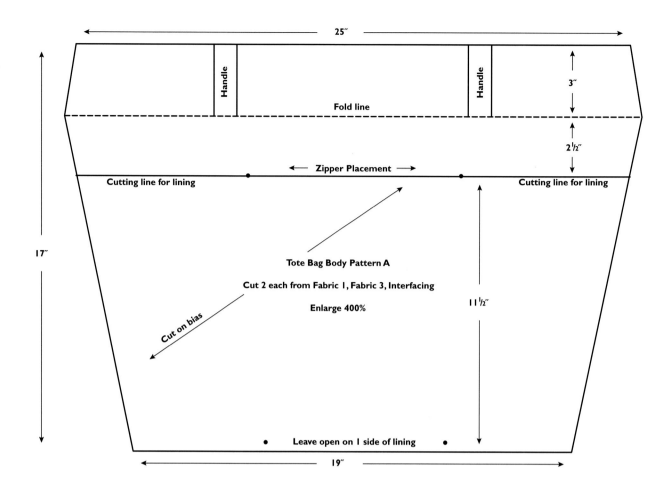

25″

Handle · Fold line · Handle

3″

2½″

17″

Zipper Placement

Cutting line for lining · Cutting line for lining

Tote Bag Body Pattern A

Cut 2 each from Fabric 1, Fabric 3, Interfacing

Enlarge 400%

Cut on bias

11½″

Leave open on 1 side of lining

19″

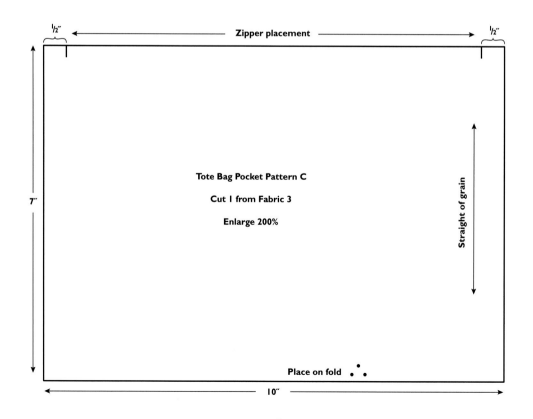

½″

Zipper placement

½″

7″

Tote Bag Pocket Pattern C

Cut 1 from Fabric 3

Enlarge 200%

Straight of grain

Place on fold

10″

a day around town

It begins as a day of errands that turns into a lunch out. Thank goodness you brought your bag that can handle whatever you stow in it. Cell phone, wallet, glasses, theater tickets, and miscellaneous papers and forms are tucked away neatly, ready for whatever life throws your way.

FINISHED SIZE: 8˝ x 6˝ x 3˝

What You'll Need

Note: Use fusible fleece with adhesive on only one side.

- ☐ ¾ yard fashion Fabric 1
- ☐ ½ yard lining, Fabric 2
- ☐ 1 yard fusible fleece
- ☐ ½ yard lightweight fusible interfacing
- ☐ 2 yards ½″ cotton piping
- ☐ 1 magnetic snap
- ☐ Matching thread

How-To's

cutting

Note: Patterns and measurements for cutting are on pages 51–52.

Cut 1 exterior pocket A each from Fabric 1, Fabric 2, and fusible fleece.

Cut 2 bag bodies B each from Fabric 1 and fusible fleece.

Cut 2 lining bodies B from Fabric 2.

Cut 2 bias strips 3″ × 17″ from Fabric 1 for handles.

Cut 2 bias strips 3″ × 17″ from fusible lightweight interfacing for handles.

Cut 1 bag bottom C each from Fabric 1, Fabric 2, and fusible fleece.

Cut 1 flap D each from Fabric 1, Fabric 2, and fusible fleece.

Cut 1 rectangle 6″ × 8″ from Fabric 2 for interior pocket.

fusing

1. Trim ½″ seam allowance from all edges of the fusible fleece.

2. Fuse the fusible fleece to the wrong side of exterior pocket A, to the wrong sides of Fabric 1, to the wrong sides of Fabric 2, and to the wrong side of flap D, and to the wrong side of bottom C.

3. Fuse the lightweight interfacing to the Fabric 1 handles.

sewing

Note: All seams are ½″, unless otherwise stated.

1. Center one part of a magnetic closure on a short end of the right side of pocket A, 1½″ from the raw edge. Apply a magnetic clasp part.

2. With rights sides together, pin around 2 long sides and the top of the pocket. Clip the corners, and trim the seam allowance to ¼″. Turn the pocket right side out and press.

3. Center pocket A on the right side of bag A, raw edges matching. Baste across the bottom edge. Edgestitch along both sides.

4. Construct a bottom wrap (pages 14).

5. Make 2 corded handles 17″ long (page 16).

easy!

Try substituting ½″ decorator cording rather than making handles.

6. Pin the raw handle edges to the bag's top edges, 2″ from each side seam. Baste.

7. Follow Steps 1 and 2 to make flap D and to add the second part of the magnetic closure.

8. Center the flap, right sides together, between the handles on the bag's back side. Baste in place.

9. Create a patch pocket for the interior (page 18).

10. Center the pocket on the right side of bag lining B, 1½˝ from the lower edge. Edgestitch the pocket in place.

11. Construct the bag's lining using the bottom wrap technique (page 14). *Be sure to leave a 5˝ opening in one lower seam.*

12. Slip the bag with right sides out into the lining, which has wrong sides out. Right sides of Fabric 1 and Fabric 2 will be together. Match the side seams. Pin in place. Stitch around the bag's top edge. Trim the seam allowance to ¼˝, clipping the curved edges as needed.

Trim and clip the top edge.

13. Turn the bag right side out. Press the lining to the bag's inside. Topstitch around the bag's upper edge.

14. Machine stitch the bag lining closed at the lower opening.

15. Hand tack the lining to the bag at the 4 bottom corners.

variation

Create a truly unique day bag by adding purchased handles, fussy cutting fabrics to maintain the fabric design, and adding some painted or stamped touches.

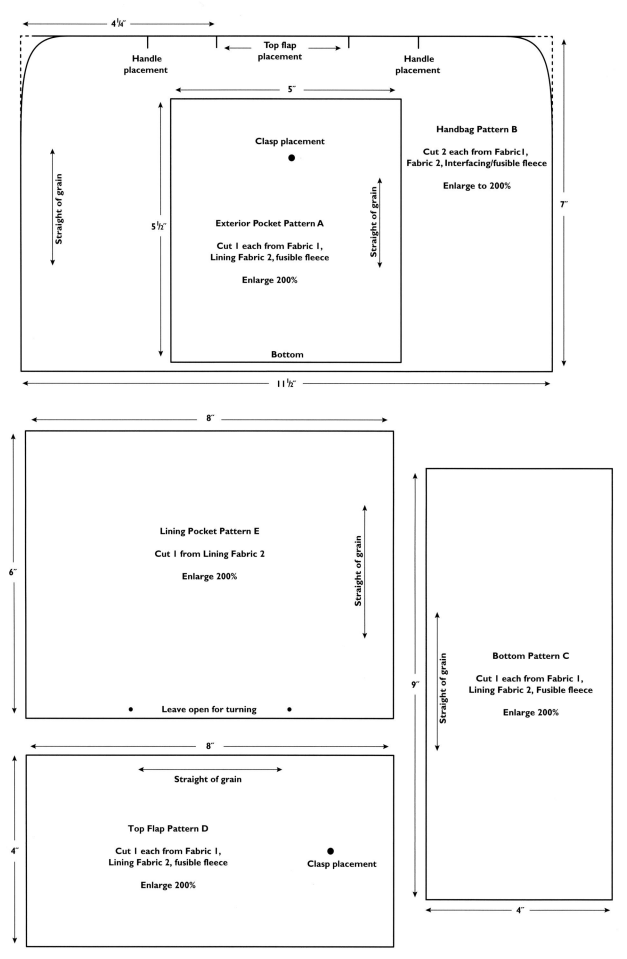

4¼″

Handle placement

Top flap placement

Handle placement

5″

Clasp placement

Straight of grain

Straight of grain

Handbag Pattern B

Cut 2 each from Fabric 1, Fabric 2, Interfacing/fusible fleece

Enlarge to 200%

7″

5½″

Exterior Pocket Pattern A

Cut 1 each from Fabric 1, Lining Fabric 2, fusible fleece

Enlarge 200%

Bottom

11½″

8″

6″

Lining Pocket Pattern E

Cut 1 from Lining Fabric 2

Enlarge 200%

Straight of grain

Leave open for turning

Bottom Pattern C

Cut 1 each from Fabric 1, Lining Fabric 2, Fusible fleece

Enlarge 200%

Straight of grain

9″

4″

8″

Straight of grain

Top Flap Pattern D

Cut 1 each from Fabric 1, Lining Fabric 2, fusible fleece

Enlarge 200%

Clasp placement

4″

4″

knitting and crafts/
market bag

Your projects or produce can be carried in style with this multipurpose bag, which can be made in a weekend. This bag features multiple inside pockets to hold everything you need. Make the needle case to corral your favorite knitting needles.

FINISHED SIZE: 17˝ x 16˝

What You'll Need

- ☐ 1¼ yard black floral, Fabric 1
- ☐ 2 yards stripe, Fabric 2
- ☐ 1 yard fusible interfacing
- ☐ ⅞ yard of 1″ grosgrain ribbon
- ☐ ⅝ yard of ⅜″ grosgrain ribbon
- ☐ 1″ button to cover

- ☐ Four 1″ D-rings
- ☐ 3¼″ × 27″ canvas
- ☐ 3¼″ × 13¼″ stiff interfacing
- ☐ Fabric glue
- ☐ Seam sealant
- ☐ Matching thread

How To's

cutting

Note: Templates for all patterns are on page 57–58. Enlarge patterns as marked.

Cut 2 A's each from Fabric 1 and interfacing for bag front and back.

Cut 1 C from Fabric 1 for the single interior pocket and 1 D from Fabric 1 for the double interior pocket.

Cut 2 B's from Fabric 2 for bag lining.

Cut 1 E from Fabric 2 for exterior pocket.

Cut 2 bias strips 2″ × 24″ from Fabric 1 and 2 from Fabric 2 for the handles.

Cut the 1″ grosgrain ribbon into 4 strips of 5″ for the handles.

Cut the ⅜″ grosgrain ribbon to a 20″ length.

Cut 2 rectangles 3¼″ × 13¼″ from the canvas.

Cut 1 rectangle 3¼″ × 13¼″ from the stiff interfacing.

fusing

1. Construct 2 flat handles (page 17) by pairing a Fabric 1 strip and a Fabric 2 strip for each handle.

2. Fuse the 4 interfacing pieces to each of the 4 handles.

3. Fuse the interfacing to the bag's front and back A.

sewing

Note: All seams are ½″, unless otherwise stated.

1. Sew the C and D interior pockets and turn right sides out. Press.

2. Sew the bag's exterior pocket E and turn right side out. Press.

3. Pin the interior pockets to the right side of the bag's lining B, placing 1 pocket on the front side of the lining and 1 pocket on the back side, along the placement lines on the pattern. To create the double pocket D, stitch vertically 3½″ parallel to the left edge of pocket D. Edgestitch in place around each pocket's side and bottom edges (see page 18).

4. Pin the top of exterior pocket E to bag front A. For the bottom edge, create a pleat at each of the pocket's bottom corners by bringing outside corners in about ⅞″ on each side and lining up the inner and outer marks. The inner marks will be on top. Pin the overlapping pleat in place. Edgestitch along the pocket sides and bottom edge.

Bottom pleat

5. Stitch bag front A to bag back A along the side seams and the bottom edge. Press seams open. Repeat for bag lining B.

6. Prepare the rings for handle placement: Take a 5″ length of 1″ grosgrain ribbon. Slide a D-ring to the middle of the ribbon, and fold the ribbon in half lengthwise. Machine baste a vertical line down the ribbon to keep the ribbon edges aligned. You will remove the basting stitches when the bag is complete.

fun!

If D-rings are not available, try a standard ring. If that is not an option, make your straps a bit longer and sew the ends at the same place as for the ribbons in step 6.

7. Secure the D-ring by using a zipper foot to stitch across the width of the ribbon close to the straight edge of the D-ring.

8. Following the placement lines, baste the raw edges of the ribbon to the raw edges of the bag's front and back. Repeat for the other 3 rings.

9. Use the 20″ piece of ⅜″ grosgrain ribbon. Keeping the same ribbon side up, fold the ribbon in half and shape it into a point. Press. Stitch across the width of the flattened ribbon just above the point. Center the ribbon between the front D-rings, following the placement lines on the pattern. With raw edges even, baste in place.

D-rings and ribbon stitched in place

10. To attach the lining to the bag, turn the lining wrong side out. Slip the bag, right side out, into the lining (right sides are facing each other). Match seamlines and handles on the placement lines; pin. Stitch around the entire bag. Trim the seam allowance. Pull the bag through the opening in the lining's bottom.

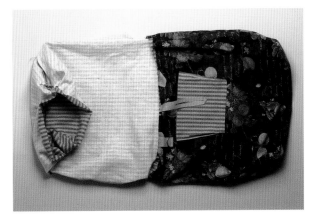

Pull bag through lining opening.

11. Tuck the lining into the bag, aligning side and bottom seams.

12. Roll the top edge of the lining to the bag top along the fold line. Press. Pin in place.

13. With a zipper foot, stitch as close as possible in the seam where the coordinating striped lining is sewn to the dark floral fabric. This is known as "stitching in-the-ditch."

14. With the precut canvas and stiff interfacing, make a "canvas sandwich" by placing the stiff interfacing between the 2 layers of canvas. Machine baste all 3 layers.

15. Test fit the bottom piece; trim if needed. Slip the bottom piece into position through the hole left in the lining between the outside of the bag and the lining, applying a layer of fabric glue inside the bag's seam before final positioning.

16. Hand stitch the lining opening closed.

17. With a heavy needle and thread, tack the lining to the bag at each of the corners.

18. Using a heavy zigzag stitch, sew over the handle raw edges.

19. Use a zigzag stitch to fold under ⅜″ on the end of the handle; press. Slip that end into the D-ring and fold it over another ⅝″. Pin in place. Stitch through all the layers a couple of times to give the handles added strength.

20. Repeat for the other handle ends, making sure that each side has both ends of the same handle. Remove the vertical basting stitches from all 4 handles.

21. Cover the 1″ button with Fabric 1, following the button manufacturer's instructions. Stitch the button to the top layer of the exterior pocket. Slip the ribbon loop over the button to keep the exterior pocket secure.

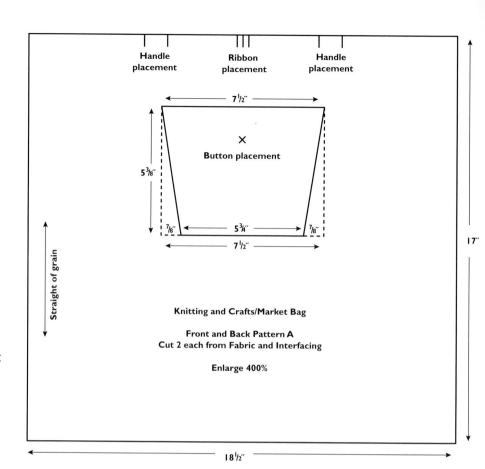

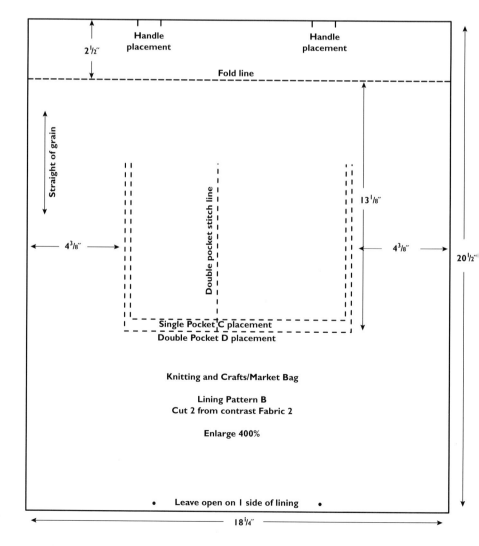

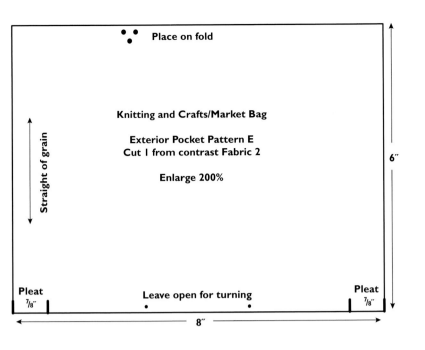

Place on fold

Knitting and Crafts/Market Bag

Exterior Pocket Pattern E
Cut 1 from contrast Fabric 2

Enlarge 200%

Straight of grain

6″

Pleat
⅞″

Leave open for turning

Pleat
⅞″

8″

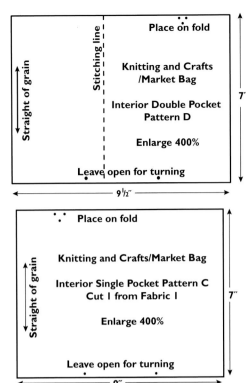

Straight of grain

Stitching line

Place on fold

Knitting and Crafts
/Market Bag

Interior Double Pocket
Pattern D

Enlarge 400%

Leave open for turning

7″

9½″

Place on fold

Knitting and Crafts/Market Bag

Interior Single Pocket Pattern C
Cut 1 from Fabric 1

Enlarge 400%

Straight of grain

Leave open for turning

7″

9″

needle case

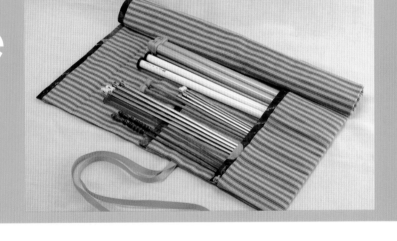

FINISHED SIZE: Unfolded 17¾″ × 18″
Folded 7″ × 15″

What You'll Need

☐ ⅞ yard stripe, Fabric 1

☐ ⅓ yard black floral, Fabric 2

☐ ⅝ yard lightweight lining, Fabric 3

☐ ⅝ yard fusible interfacing

☐ 1⅙ yards ⅜″ ribbon

How-To's

cutting

Cut 1 A from Fabric 1.

Cut 1 B from Fabric 1.

Cut 1 C from Fabric 3.

Cut 1 D from Fabric 1 (and interfacing, if using).

To make piping, cut 3 bias strips 2″ × 19″ from Fabric 2.

Cut ⅜″ grosgrain to a 40″ length.

sewing

Note: All seams are ½″, unless otherwise stated.

1. Prepare 3 bias strips by folding in ⅝″ on each short end. Press into place. Trim ¼″ from the turned-under edge.

Apply bias piping.

2. Fold each long strip in half, wrong sides together, so the piece measures 1″ wide.

3. Pin the bias strip at the top and bottom of the case back A. Make sure that each end measures ½″ in from each seam allowance. Baste in place using a ⅜″ seam allowance. Repeat for the top edge of the needle case pocket D.

4. Stitch front facing B to the top of front lining C. Leave a 4″ opening in the seam. Press the seam up.

5. Matching the notches, stitch the bottom edge of lining C to the top edge of front pocket D, sandwiching the piping. Turn the pocket to the right side, and press seams down, away from the piping.

6. With right sides together, match the notches and pin case back A to the top edge of facing B. Stitch together.

7. Stitch the lower edge of case back A to the bottom edge of front pocket D, matching notches. Turn the bag right side out. Press seams down, away from the piping.

Bring pocket side up.

8. With the right side of the bag pocket up, position the bag facing at the top. To form an inside pocket, bring the lining seams together so they are on top of each other. Pin in place.

Lining seams matched up; ribbon positioned

9. Fold the ribbon to measure 17″ on one side and 23″ on the other. Place the fold next to the raw edge of front pocket D. Baste together the lining and the front pocket edges.

10. Turn the bag with right sides facing. Pin the side seam edges together, being careful to keep the piping free.

11. Stitch the side seams, catching the ribbon fold. Trim the corners and side seams. Apply seam sealant to the corners, and let dry. Turn the bag to the right side by pulling it through the 4″ opening in the lining seam.

12. Press the bag flat and hand stitch the lining opening closed.

13. Turn up 4½″ from the bottom edge along the fold line. Press. Unfold the flap and use a contrasting thread to baste along the fold line.

14. Using pattern D as your guide, mark stitch lines to form individual, vertical pockets. Start stitching just below the piped edge to the basting line. *Stitched spaces between the lines can be altered to meet your needs.*

15. Fold the bottom up to form a lower, horizontal pocket. Pin in place. Edgestitch on each side of the lower pocket to keep it in place. Repeat Step 14. Note the pocket size differences. Remove the basting stitch.

16. Apply a drop of seam sealant to each ribbon end to prevent unraveling.

17. To close your case, begin by folding the top down 3″ from the edge. Press in place. This secures your needles when your case is rolled up.

18. Fold the case in thirds, lengthwise, and secure with the ribbon tie.

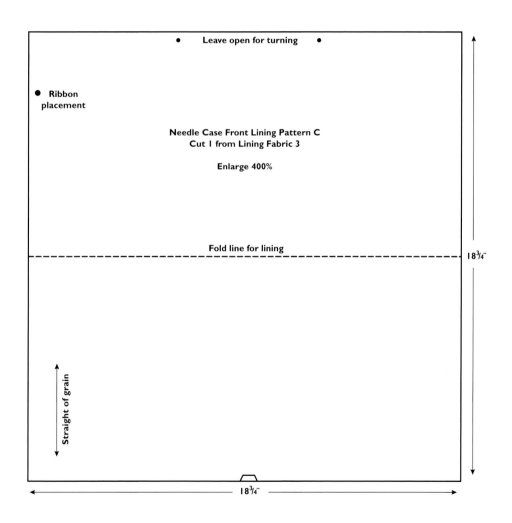

Leave open for turning

● Ribbon placement

Needle Case Front Lining Pattern C
Cut 1 from Lining Fabric 3

Enlarge 400%

Fold line for lining

18¾″

Straight of grain

18¾″

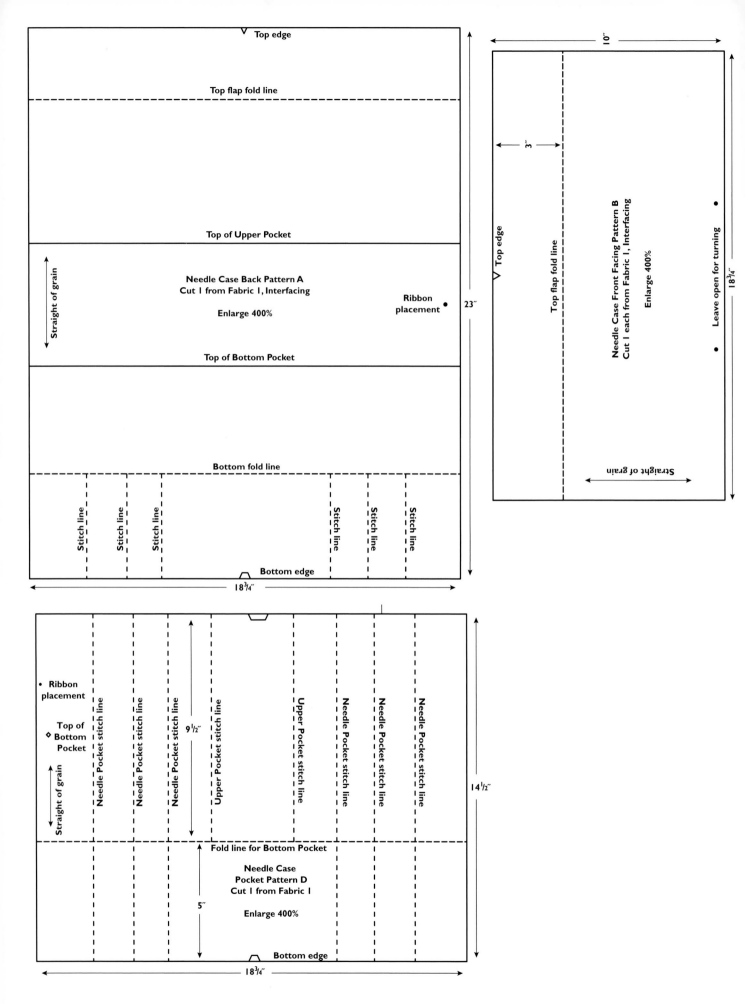

Top edge

Top flap fold line

Top of Upper Pocket

Needle Case Back Pattern A
Cut 1 from Fabric 1, Interfacing

Enlarge 400%

Ribbon
placement

Straight of grain

Top of Bottom Pocket

23″

Bottom fold line

Stitch line   Stitch line   Stitch line   Stitch line   Stitch line   Stitch line

Bottom edge

18¾″

10″

3″

Top edge

Top flap fold line

Needle Case Front Facing Pattern B
Cut 1 each from Fabric 1, Interfacing

Enlarge 400%

Leave open for turning

Straight of grain

18¾″

Ribbon
placement

Top of
Bottom
Pocket

Straight of grain

Needle Pocket stitch line   Needle Pocket stitch line   Needle Pocket stitch line   Upper Pocket stitch line   Upper Pocket stitch line   Needle Pocket stitch line   Needle Pocket stitch line   Needle Pocket stitch line

9½″

14½″

Fold line for Bottom Pocket

Needle Case
Pocket Pattern D
Cut 1 from Fabric 1

Enlarge 400%

5″

Bottom edge

18¾″

fun and easy
embellishments

Embellishments are the special add-ons that readily transform your bag into a personal statement. Add one or more of these stylized techniques to any bag surface to create a one-of-a-kind work of art.

easy!

Couching Yarns and Ribbons

lazy yarns ready for "the couch"

Imagine a piece of fabric with yarns and ribbons leisurely wandering its surface. This is the concept behind couching. Apply trims after you have interfaced the bag for stability but before you stitch the bag together. Couching is so simple, it *can't* be done wrong.

Start with a colorful yarn, ribbon, or embroidery floss that complements the bag fabric. Add a simple zigzag stitch slightly wider than the yarn. Stitch the yarn in place, allowing it to meander. It's as easy as that.

For a yarn that looks like it is floating on the surface, use a clear monofilament thread as the top thread and a matching fabric thread in the bobbin. For additional dimension, or drama, consider zigzagging over the yarn with a contrasting or metallic thread. You can also repeat these steps with additional colors or different ribbons, floss and yarns, or layer upon layer. The hard part is determining when to stop.

Red couched bag

fast!

Faux couching can also be done with fabric glue. Use a light bead of fabric glue to draw the positioning lines on the bag's right side. Quickly and gently finger-press the ribbons or yarns into place. Be sure to select a glue that will not soak through your trim. Allow the bag to dry before moving it.

Beaded Fringe or Hand Beading

bead-azzle them

Whereas couched threads and yarns add dimension, beads add dazzle. Beads range in size from very small seed beads, which are applied with a fine hand-beading needle, to larger sizes, which a sewing machine needle can go through. Larger beads can also be threaded on yarn, ribbon, or other trim.

Before beading, be sure to stabilize fabric with interfacing. It is easier to apply seed beads before sewing the lining into the bag. Although you can apply seed beads after the bag is completed, extra attention is required to prevent accidentally catching the lining with the beading stitches. Always apply machine-sewn beads before sewing the bag together. Remember, machine sewing features a decorative thread and is faster than hand stitching, but pay close attention to avoid needle breakage.

It's a good idea to take along a sewing machine needle when shopping for machine-applied beads. Use it as a guide when selecting beads. If the needle goes through the bead opening, you can expect a good fit through the bead hole when you are machine stitching. Typically, a size 8 or 10 bead will accommodate a standard machine needle. Always buy a few more beads than the project calls for. If there is an irregular hole or if a needle hits a bead, you will still have enough beads to complete the work.

For a softer look, sew machine-applied beads with an open-toe presser foot with a monofilament or matching thread. For added embellishment, consider using a contrasting or metallic thread with a stitch pattern that will enhance the overall look of the project. You can sew beads with straight, curved, or patterned stitches. The trick is to *take your time* as you apply the bead.

Take a few preliminary stitches, then stop sewing with the needle down in the fabric. Lift the presser foot. Place the bead, hole side up, exactly where you want to stitch it. Hold the bead with your fingers or a pair of tweezers. Manually turn the handwheel to stitch the bead into place. Take a couple more stitches so the bead clears the presser foot before lowering the foot and increasing your sewing speed. Before you know it, a wonderful web of stitches and beads will adorn your bag.

Another choice is ready-made beaded fringe, which lets you have all the glamour without all the work. Beaded fringe offers two placement options: either applying it before the lining is attached and catching the ribbon header in the seam allowance, or sewing it with a single or double row of stitches to the top of a completed bag.

fast!

If the beaded fringe has been sewn too close to the seam, break the closest bead with a pair of pliers and remove the fragments.

easy!

Glue beaded fringe to the top of the bag by running a narrow line of glue exactly where the trim is to be placed. Arrange the trim carefully and apply pressure as you go. Lay flat to dry.

For a speedy dose of bead-azzlement, how about trying a heated applicator wand? This handy device picks up a preglued crystal with a heated tip and activates the glue as the crystal is applied. It also lets you put the beads exactly where you want them.

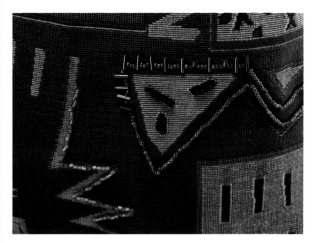

Blue beaded bag

Appliqués

fusible fun

Appliqué is a fun and easy way to add special motifs to your bag surface. Thanks to paper-backed fusible web, any fabric becomes a potential motif. This fast method allows for a specific fabric section to be fused to a bag surface before the bag is sewn. Here's how.

1. Start by selecting the motif to be featured.

2. Apply paper-backed fusible web to the wrong side of the motif area, allowing an extra inch beyond the planned edge. Let the motif cool thoroughly before moving.

3. Carefully cut around the motif, leaving an extra ¼″ all around it.

Appliqué adds interesting detail.

4. Test the position of the motif on the right side of the bag. Peel off the paper backing and fuse in place.

5. Finish the edges with satin stitching—this dense zigzag stitch covers the raw edges of the motif.

Add seed beads to highlight the motif's special features.

Embroidery

hoop, hoop hooray!

Embroidery, whether by hand or machine, offers a wide range of pattern, color, and texture options. Hand embroidery is highly portable. You can easily slip it in a bag and take it along. Machine embroidery creates a programmed design that can be sewn while you answer the phone or work on another project nearby. In both cases, embroidery is applied after the interfacing but before the bag is sewn.

Some tasks are common to both hand and machine embroidery: determining the stitch placement, selecting the right thread and needle, and using the correct hooping technique.

There are a variety of thread types for both embroidery methods—some require stabilization of the base fabric, others do not. Consult your sewing machine manual or an embroidery book for specific instructions on hand and machine techniques, hooping, and stabilization.

Once your design has been embroidered, lightly press it face, down on, a plush towel to set the stitches into the fabric.

easy!

For optimal positioning, stitch a machine-embroidered design on a larger piece of interfaced fabric *before* you cut out the bag.

From ribbons to floss to metallic threads, whether stitched by hand or machine, embroidery offers an easy means of adding surface interest and texture.

Lavender embroidered bag

Stamping

stamp out boring fabric

If lackluster fabric is hurting your project, bring it to life with a fast application of color and design delivered by stamping. You have control over the selection of color and theme, as well as the density the fabric requires. Give your bag a magical makeover with stamping—before or after the bag is made.

Try stamping on lining fabric to create internal interest.

Even the most basic, least interesting pieces can find new purpose with a splash of color in a fun, new design. Basic gray linen develops a new attitude when black swirls are added. Even the "wrong" fabric color bought several seasons ago can be updated with healthy doses of layered brights or neutrals.

fun!

Watch upscale clothing catalogs for stamping inspiration.

The key point is to practice! To do that, you will need some extra bag fabric, textile paints, a small paint container, stamps or sponges cut into interesting designs, and paper towels. Once the stamp or sponge has been loaded with paint, give a trial press on a paper towel to absorb excess paint. This will ensure that you leave a crisp design on your fabric.

easy!

Plan to spend time perfecting your stamping techniques and plotting placement of the motifs.

With practice, your stamping rhythm, as well as a new fabric, will develop. If additional colors are part of the fabric's new design, provide ample drying time between applications.

fast!

Start stamping from the top down, moving the freshly stamped work out of harm's way.

Imagine all the fun you can have with these five fun and easy embellishment methods. They open up a whole new spectrum of possibilities. Experimenting with two or more techniques quickly yields a multidimensional effect. For example, stamp the bag, add a touch of embroidery, and add seed beads for more texture. Try one, then another and another. Remember, *experimenting is good for you and your creativity!*

About the Author

Pam Archer hails from Portland, Oregon, and is a wife and the mother of two sons. As a child, she played for hours at a time with fabric scraps. When introduced to sewing, she fell in love with it.

With a bachelor's degree in clothing and textiles, Pam began her career in retail management. She later freelanced as a national spokesperson for a major pattern company and furthered her career by developing a high-school fashion marketing program.

Pam enjoys seeing fabric and texture take on their own form and life. Her greatest satisfaction comes from creating items that evoke a sense of delight in others.

Resources

Look for bag-making supplies at your local fabric, craft, and quilt shops. Bag-making supplies are also available from the following mail-order sources:

Clotilde LLC
P.O. Box 7500
Big Sandy, TX 75755-7500
(800) 772-2891
www.clotilde.com

Ghee's
2620 Centenary Boulevard
#2-250
Shreveport, LA 71104
(318) 226-1701
www.ghees.com

JoAnn Stores
www.joann.com

M&J Trimming
1000 Sixth Avenue
New York, NY 10018
(800) 9-MJTRIM
www.mjtrim.com

Nancy's Notions
333 Beichl Avenue
Beaver Dam, WI 53916
(800) 833-0690
www.nancysnotions.com

UMX—Universal Mercantile Exchange
21128 Commerce Point Drive
Walnut Creek, CA 91789
(800) 755-6608
www.umei.com

stiff interfacing

Stiff interfacings, such as fast2fuse and Timtex, are available from Clotilde (see above) and these shops:

Web of Thread
18208 66th Avenue NE
Suite 102
Kenmore, WA 98028
(800) 955-8185
www.webofthread.com

Fabric.com
2151 Northwest Parkway
Suite 500
Marietta, GA 30067
(888) 455-2940
www.fabric.com

3-in-1 Color Tool
fast2fuse
C&T Publishing, Inc.

For more information, ask for a free catalog:
C&T Publishing, Inc.
P.O. Box 1456
Lafayette, CA 94549
(800) 284-1114
Email:ctinfo@ctpub.com
Website: www.ctpub.com

For quilting supplies:
Cotton Patch Mail Order
3405 Hall Lane, Dept. CTB
Lafayette, CA 94549
(800) 835-4418
(925) 283-7883
Email: quiltusa@yahoo.com
Website: www.quiltusa.com